DATE DUE

Demco, Inc. 38-293

Brazil

by Tracey Boraas

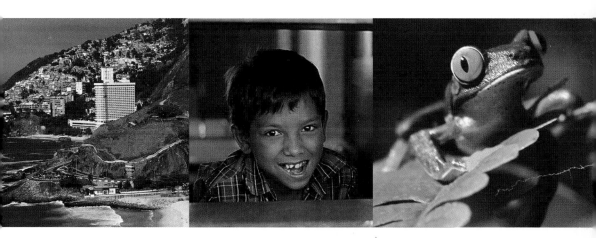

Content Consultant:
Colin M. MacLachlan
John Christy Barr Distinguished Professor of History
Professor of Brazilian Studies, Tulane University
Reading Consultant:
Dr. Robert Miller, Professor of Special Education
Minnesota State University, Mankato

Bridgestone Books
an imprint of Capstone Press
Mankato, Minnesota

Bridgestone Books are published by Capstone Press
151 Good Counsel Drive, P.O. Box 669, Mankato, Minnesota 56002
http://www.capstone-press.com

Library of Congress Cataloging-in-Publication Data
Boraas, Tracey.
    Brazil/by Tracey Boraas.
    p. cm.—(Countries and cultures)
    Includes bibliographical references and index.
    ISBN 0-7368-0765-9
    1. Brazil—Juvenile literature. [1. Brazil.] I. Title. II. Series.
F2508.5 .B57 2002
981—dc21   00-009829

Summary: An introduction to the geography, history, economy, culture, and
people of Brazil.

Editorial Credits
Connie R. Colwell and Gillia M. Olson, editors; Lois Wallentine, product
    planning editor; Heather Kindseth, graphic designer; Kia Bielke, illustrator;
    Katy Kudela, photo researcher

Photo Credits
Archive Photos, 24, 28; Betty Crowell, 39; DAVID R. FRAZIER Photolibrary, 1
(center), 23, 46, 63; Digital Stock, cover (right), 1 (left, right); Digital Vision,
56; Doris J. Brookes, 4; FPG International LLC/TravelPix, 17; Gary
Milburn/TOM STACK & ASSOCIATES, 13; Gary Sundermeyer/Capstone
Press, 51; International Stock/Paulo Fridman, 42; North Wind Picture Archives,
20, 27; One Mile Up, Inc., 57 (both); Photo Network/Bonnie Flamer, 15; Photo
Network/Luke Potter, 45; Reuters/Vanderlei Almeida/Archive Photos, 32;
Reuters/Paulo Whitaker/Archive Photos, 52; Root Resources/Roger J. Naser, 54;
Telegraph Colour Library/FPG International LLC, cover (left), 18–19; TRIP/J.
Drew, 8; TRIP/S. Grant, 34; Visuals Unlimited/William Dunwiddle, 31; Visuals
Unlimited/Gilbert Twiest, 48–49

Artistic Effects
Capstone Press, Digital Stock, Photodisc, Inc., PictureQuest

Contents

Fast Facts about Brazil

Name: Federative Republic of Brazil; Republica Federativa do Brasil

Location: Eastern South America, bordering the Atlantic Ocean

Bordering countries and waters: Argentina, Bolivia, Colombia, French Guiana, Guyana, Paraguay, Peru, Suriname, Uruguay, Venezuela, and the Atlantic Ocean

National population: 171,853,126

Capital: Brasília

Major cities and populations: São Paulo (10,017,821), Rio de Janeiro (5,606,497), Belo Horizonte (2,097,311), Brasília (1,737,813)

Explore Brazil

South America's largest country, Brazil is home to the world's largest wetland area. The Pantanal is a huge swamp in western Brazil. The wetland covers about 77,000 square miles (199,430 square kilometers). Summer rains flood the area. The floodwaters create shallow lakes and carry fertile soil across the wetland.

The Pantanal is famous for its wide variety of plants and wildlife. Trees and tall grasses thrive throughout the wetland. Alligators, caimans, anacondas, spider monkeys, and gibbons make their homes in the Pantanal. Hundreds of tropical birds fly over the area, and many fish dwell in the region's lakes and rivers. Visitors can explore the Pantanal in canoes and can view wildlife from above in small planes and hot-air balloons.

◀ Caimans swim through the swamps of the Pantanal in western Brazil. They are related to alligators and crocodiles.

The Giant in South America

The Pantanal is only part of Brazil's vast landscape. As the fifth largest country in the world, Brazil is a giant among nations. The country occupies nearly half of South America, covering 3,286,470 square miles (8,511,965 square kilometers). Only Russia, Canada, China, and the United States are larger than Brazil.

Brazil borders the Atlantic Ocean on the east and 10 countries to the north, west, and south. Venezuela, Guyana, Suriname, and French Guiana lie to the north. Colombia is Brazil's northwestern neighbor. Peru, Bolivia, and Paraguay border Brazil to the west. Brazil shares boundaries with Argentina to the southwest and Uruguay to the south. In fact, Brazil shares boundaries with every South American country except Ecuador and Chile.

Brazil also is a giant in population, ranking fifth in the world. More than 170 million people call Brazil home. Only China, India, the United States, and Indonesia have larger populations than Brazil. Most of Brazil's people live in cities along the eastern coast.

COLOMBIA

VENEZUELA

GUYANA

SURINAME

FRENCH
GUIANA

Roraima

Amapá

N
W   E
S

ECUADOR

Amazonas

Pará

Maranhão

Ceará

Rio Grande
do Norte

PERU

Acre

Piauí

Paraíba

Rondônia

Tocantins

Pernambuco

Recife ●

Mato Grosso

Bahia

Alagoas

Maceió ●

BOLIVIA

Distrito Federal

Brasília ✪

Sergipe

Salvador ●

PACIFIC
OCEAN

Goiás

Minas
Gerais

Mato
Grosso do
Sul

Belo Horizonte ●

Espírito
Santo

CHILE

São Paulo

Rio de Janeiro

PARAGUAY

Paraná

São Paulo ●

Rio de Janeiro ●

ARGENTINA

Santa Catarina

ATLANTIC
OCEAN

Scale
Miles

100 200 300 400

Rio Grande
do Sul

150 300 450 600
Kilometers

URUGUAY

Geopolitical Map of Brazil

KEY
✪ CAPITAL
● CITIES

Fast Facts about Brazil's Land

Area: 3,286,470 square miles (8,511,965 square kilometers)

Latitude and longitude of geographic center: 10 degrees south latitude, 55 degrees west longitude

Highest elevation: Pico da Neblina, 9,888 feet (3,014 meters)

Lowest elevation: Atlantic Ocean, sea level

Chapter 2

The Land, Climate, and Wildlife

Brazil can be divided into five land regions. These areas are the central region, the northeastern region, the southeastern region, the southern region, and the Amazon Rain Forest. Each of these areas has different land features, climate, and wildlife.

The Central Region

Brazil's central region is home to the country's capital of Brasília. This city has almost 2 million people.

The central region lies almost entirely on the Central Plateau. This high, flat area is covered mostly by scrub brush and trees, but rich soil lies beneath the vegetation.

The Pantanal also is part of Brazil's central region. During the rainy season, the Paraguay River overflows its banks from October to April, creating this wetland.

◀ Dense brush covers the northern area of Mato Grosso in the central region.

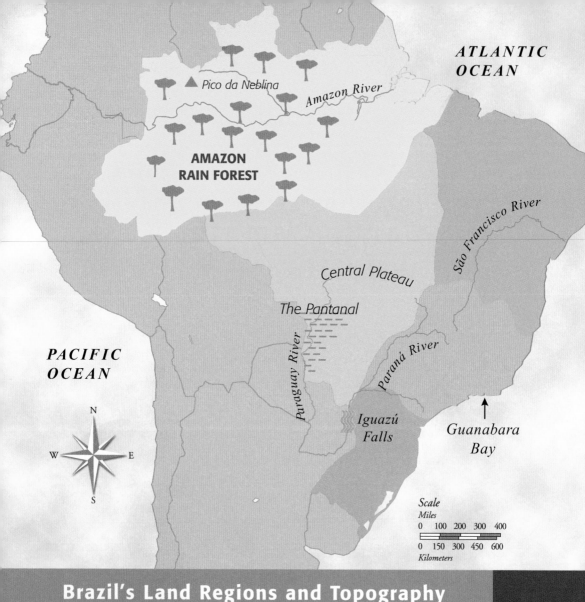

ATLANTIC
OCEAN

Pico da Neblina

Amazon River

AMAZON
RAIN FOREST

São Francisco River

Central Plateau

The Pantanal

PACIFIC
OCEAN

Paraguay River

Paraná River

Iguazú
Falls

Guanabara
Bay

N
W   E
S

Scale
Miles
0   100   200   300   400

0   150   300   450   600
Kilometers

Brazil's Land Regions and Topography

KEY

Central Region

Northeastern Region

Southeastern Region

Southern Region

Amazon Rain Forest Region

Pantanal

Rain Forest

Rivers

Mountain

More than 350 types of fish and 600 species of birds live in the Pantanal. These birds include ibis, macaws, egrets, and cuckoos.

The Central Plateau has moderate weather. Temperatures average about 79 degrees Fahrenheit (26 degrees Celsius) during the summer and 73 degrees Fahrenheit (23 degrees Celsius) in the winter. The region usually receives between 40 and 70 inches (102 and 178 centimeters) of rainfall each year.

The Northeastern Region

Coastal lowlands cover much of the northeastern region. White sandy beaches bordered by sand dunes stretch along the shoreline. In some areas, coral reefs lie just offshore. Lagoons often lie between the beaches and the coral reefs. To the west, the land changes to wetland and level plains.

The weather in the northeastern region usually is warm and sunny. The average temperature is 84 degrees Fahrenheit (29 degrees Celsius), but temperatures can reach more than 100 degrees Fahrenheit (38 degrees Celsius). Inland areas are dry and experience frequent droughts. The northeastern region receives between 15 and 30 inches (38 and 76 centimeters) of rain each year.

The plant life in the northeastern region changes from east to west. Palm trees and tropical plants such as cocoa and sugarcane grow along the beaches. Cactus, shrub brush, and caatinga bush lie farther inland. These plants, which need little water, flourish in the dry inland climate.

About 30 percent of Brazil's population lives in the northeastern region. Many people make their homes in cities such as Recife, Maceió, and Salvador, which are known for beautiful beaches and interesting historical sites.

The northeastern region is home to one major river, the São Francisco. The São Francisco is about 1,800 miles (2,900 kilometers) long and is the region's major source of transportation, water, and energy.

The Southeastern Region

The southeastern region is home to most of the country's large cities. Although it covers only 11 percent of Brazil's land, the region includes the country's three largest cities—São Paulo, Rio de Janeiro, and Belo Horizonte. More than 44 percent of Brazil's population lives in the southeastern region. The moderate climate creates excellent conditions for farming and industrial development. A large plateau

▼ Rio de Janeiro, the second largest city in Brazil, is located in the southeastern region.

covers most of the region, which has excellent farmland for growing coffee.

Rio de Janeiro is one of the most important cities in Brazil. Brazilians call this city the "cidade maravilhosa," which means marvelous city. The famous Sugar Loaf Mountain lies just off the coast of Rio de Janeiro in Guanabara Bay. Beaches such as Copacabana and Ipanema line the shore. Tourists travel from all over the world to visit Rio de Janeiro.

Southern Region

The southern region has the most varied landscape in Brazil. Beaches, islands, and lagoons line a narrow coastal strip along the Atlantic Ocean. A large prairie area called the pampas lies toward the country's southernmost tip. Farmers grow coffee and grain in the rich farmland of the pampas. Large herds of cattle graze on the region's prairie grasses.

The Paraná River flows through the southern region. This 3,030-mile-long (4,875-kilometer-long) river includes Iguazú Falls, a large system of waterfalls that sits at the point where Brazil meets Argentina and Paraguay.

The southern region is the only region of Brazil that experiences a change in seasons. Near the coast, the average temperature is 70 degrees Fahrenheit (21 degrees Celsius) year-round. Summer temperatures are hot in the lower elevations but can drop below

▲ Iguazú Falls lie on the Paraná River in Brazil's southern region.

72 degrees Fahrenheit (22 degrees Celsius) in higher elevations. During winter, snow sometimes falls in the higher elevations. The southern region receives about 81 inches (206 centimeters) of snow per year.

The region's moderate climate supports a variety of trees and plants. Needle-leafed pine trees, such as the Paraná pine, cover the highlands. Grasses cover the sea-level plains.

Brazil's southern region once was home to a wide variety of animal life. But much of the forest that supported monkeys, parrots, and other animals has been destroyed. These animals now mainly are found in Brazilian zoos. Today, the land is used as pasture for grazing cattle.

The Amazon Rain Forest Region

The world's largest tropical rain forest lies in the Amazon region. The dense, green Amazon Rain Forest stretches more than 2 million square miles (5.1 million square kilometers) across northwestern Brazil. The country's highest point, Pico da Neblina, also is in the Amazon region. This mountain is 9,888 feet (3,014 meters) tall.

▲ The Amazon River winds its way through the dense rain forest of the Amazon region.

The Amazon Rain Forest is warm and wet. The region receives an average of 78 inches (198 centimeters) of rain each year. In some areas, more than 160 inches (406 centimeters) of rain falls each year. The Amazon region's temperatures average between 72 and 79 degrees Fahrenheit (22 and 26 degrees Celsius).

The rain forest's hot, wet climate supports a greater variety of plants and animals than any other place on Earth. Trees such as the Brazil nut, the mahogany, the rosewood, the acacia, and the Amazonian cedar thrive in the humid air. The rain forest is home to more than 1,500 species of birds, including toucans, parrots, and hawks. About 30 types of monkeys swing from trees. Jaguars, sloths, and anteaters roam the forest floor. Scientists believe that as many as 30 million different kinds of insects live in the forest. As many as 3,000 species of fish swim in the region's rivers.

The Amazon River, the world's largest river in volume, winds through the forest. This river is 4,000 miles (6,400 kilometers) long. Scientists estimate that the Amazon River carries about 20 percent of all of the water that runs off Earth's surface.

Protecting the Rain Forest

During the 1900s, the Amazon Rain Forest began to shrink dramatically. Brazil's growing population cleared the forest to build towns and roads, plant crops, and dig for minerals. Logging companies cut down trees to make lumber. Some scientists estimate that between 1979 and 1990, the Amazon Rain Forest was destroyed at the rate of 5.4 million acres (2,185,380 hectares) per year.

In the 1990s, Brazil's government and many environmental organizations began working to protect the Amazon Rain Forest. They also provide education about how to make money from the rain forest without damaging it. Many people now harvest nuts, fruits, rubber, and other products that grow naturally in the rain forest. They often make more money than they would by clearing the land and planting crops. While rain forest destruction continues, many Brazilians believe limiting this destruction should be the country's top priority.

▲ The Amazon Rain Forest supports more types of plants and animals than any other place on Earth.

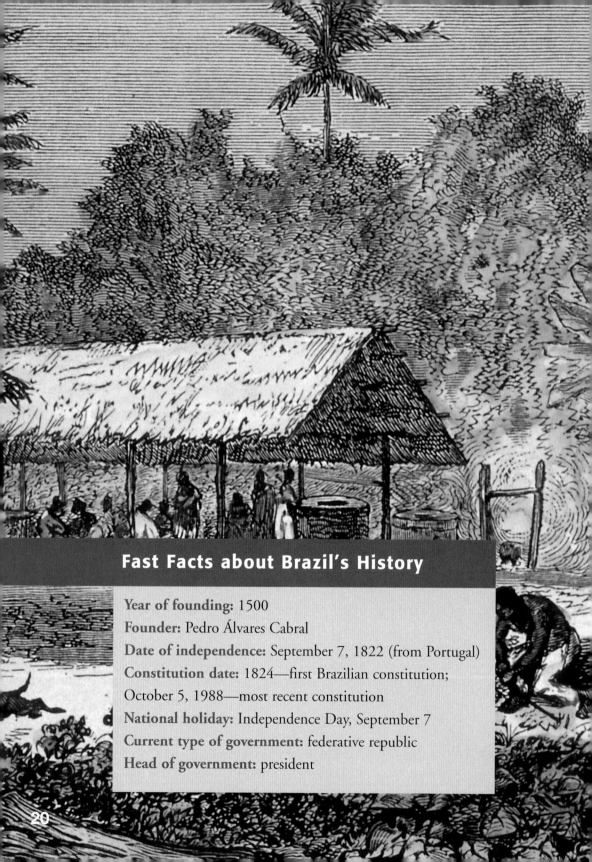

Fast Facts about Brazil's History

Year of founding: 1500

Founder: Pedro Álvares Cabral

Date of independence: September 7, 1822 (from Portugal)

Constitution date: 1824—first Brazilian constitution;
October 5, 1988—most recent constitution

National holiday: Independence Day, September 7

Current type of government: federative republic

Head of government: president

Brazil's History and Government

Scientists believe that people first arrived in South America from Asia many thousands of years ago. They probably crossed a land bridge that once connected Russia and Alaska. Some of these people settled in North America. Others moved farther south into Central America and South America.

Most of Brazil's first people were nomads. They traveled from place to place to find grazing land for their livestock. Scientists call these people Paleo-American Indians. Another group called the tropical forest Indians developed later. These people farmed and fished for a living.

European Explorers

In the A.D. 1400s, explorers from Spain and Portugal first arrived in North America and South America.

◀ Some of Brazil's first people built large log homes with dried thatched roofs.

The two European countries fought for control of this land for many years. In 1494, Spain and Portugal agreed to the Treaty of Tordesillas. The treaty divided the land in North America and South America by an imaginary line called the Line of Tordesillas. All land west of the line belonged to Spain. The land east of the line belonged to Portugal.

On April 22, 1500, the Portuguese explorer Pedro Álvares Cabral landed on Brazil's shore. This land was east of the Line of Tordesillas, so Cabral claimed it for Portugal. No Europeans yet lived in Brazil's interior. This land was west of the Line of Tordesillas and belonged to Spain.

Many Portuguese explorers soon followed Cabral, settling at trading posts along the coast. Here, they exchanged goods with the native peoples. The native peoples introduced the Portuguese to a tree called pau-brasil, which had bark that could be made into a bright red dye. The Portuguese called the tree "blazing wood," or brazilwood. Brazil was named for this tree.

The Colonial Period

Portugal appointed a colonial government in Brazil in 1549. The colonial government followed the orders of the Portuguese king.

The earliest Portuguese settlements in the colony were Salvador and Recife on the northeastern coast.

▼ The statue of the Bandeirantes honors the first explorers to establish Portuguese borders far inland.

Settlers built large sugarcane plantations in these areas. The settlers needed workers to help with the plantations. The Portuguese brought slaves from inland areas they had begun to explore. They forced native peoples to become slaves and work in the fields. Many of these native peoples became sick and died from diseases brought by the European settlers.

European missionaries began to fight slave owners and traders for control of the native peoples. The missionaries hoped to teach the native peoples about

◄ King Philip II of Spain united Spain and Portugal under his rule in 1578, making Brazil his territory.

Christianity. In the late 1500s, the missionaries won control of the native peoples. Settlers only were allowed to enslave native peoples whom they had captured in war.

Settlers then turned to the African slave market for workers. Slave traders began bringing West Africans to Brazil. Plantation owners bought the slaves and forced them to work long hours in the sugarcane fields.

In 1578, the Portuguese king, Sebastian, died and was replaced by Philip II of Spain. Philip II united Spain and Portugal under his rule. The Portuguese in Brazil later gained their independence from Spain in 1640 and claimed their land for Portugal. This land was west of the Line of Tordesillas, but Spain did not try to reclaim this territory.

In the late 1600s, people discovered gold in the city of Ouro Preto, 150 miles (241 kilometers) north of Rio de Janeiro. Many people began to travel to other areas of Brazil in search of gold. This valuable mineral soon became the main source of wealth for the country.

Kings and Emperors

A sense of unity began to grow among Brazilians in the late 1700s. Many Brazilians felt strongly that they could govern themselves. They revolted against Portuguese rule in 1789, but their revolt failed.

In 1807, France invaded Portugal. Fearing for his safety, Portuguese heir to the throne Prince Dom John sailed with his family and other nobles to Brazil. In 1815, Dom John united Brazil and Portugal as the United Kingdom of Brazil and Portugal, granting Brazil and Portugal equal power. This change opened Brazilian harbors to trade from all friendly countries. Dom John also created banks, schools, military academies, and libraries throughout Brazil.

In 1816, Queen Maria I of Portugal died. Dom John took over the Portuguese throne as King John VI. But he still wanted to oversee the new programs he had set up in Brazil. He left behind his son, Prince Dom Pedro, to rule Brazil when he returned to Portugal in 1821.

Without King John VI in Brazil, tensions there increased. A group of Brazilians called the Cortes at Lisbon were strongly in favor of keeping ties with Portugal. This group feared that Prince Dom Pedro would grant Brazilian independence. The Cortes at Lisbon tried to force Prince Dom Pedro to return to Portugal. Dom Pedro refused, and on September 7, 1822, he declared Brazil an independent nation. The Brazilian people named him Emperor Pedro I.

Pedro I made many advances in Brazil, including the approval of the country's constitution. But the emperor's popularity declined when he lost a portion of Brazil to Argentina during a costly war. That area became Uruguay. The Brazilian people became increasingly unhappy with the emperor.

Only nine years after he became emperor, Pedro I gave up his throne and returned to Portugal. He left behind his five-year-old son, Dom Pedro. When Dom

Emperor Pedro II (left) was exiled from Brazil in 1889 after a military revolt.

Pedro was 15 years old, he became Pedro II, Emperor of Brazil. Pedro II was the nation's first Brazilian-born leader.

Pedro II ruled Brazil for 49 years. He brought order to the country. He began a public school system and built factories and railroads. But he lost support from landowners when he abolished slavery. Large landowners had been his biggest supporters. Without them, he was unable to stop a revolt. In 1889, the military overthrew Pedro II.

Getúlio Vargas led
a revolt that helped
him become
Brazil's president.

Stability and Conflict

Brazil became the Republic of the United States
of Brazil in 1889. That year, the country elected
Deodoro da Fonseca as president. Brazil adopted its first
Republic Constitution in 1891. Until the 1920s, Brazil
experienced economic progress and industrial growth.

The states of São Paulo and Minas Gerais became important economic centers during this period of growth. Wealthy landowners in these states grew large amounts of coffee. They became the country's elite and controlled the government.

But in 1929, an economic crisis hit the world. The prices of coffee and other goods suddenly fell. The rich coffee plantation owners of São Paulo then insisted that a candidate from their own state be elected president. They thought a president from their state would be sympathetic to their economic problems. A revolt broke out against this presidential candidate. The revolt was led by Getúlio Vargas, the governor of the state of Rio Grande do Sul.

Getúlio Vargas

In 1934, Getúlio Vargas officially was elected president of Brazil. Vargas created a new constitution. He took away some of the power from the rich coffee states and put it in the hands of the government. This change gave Brazilian workers shorter work hours and higher wages. It also gave women the right to vote. But in 1937, Vargas wrote another constitution that took away many of these freedoms. He ruled with complete control of the country, believing his actions would bring back Brazil's stability.

During World War II (1939–1945), Vargas and his government supported the United States, declaring war against Germany and Italy. Shortly after the war, Brazilian military officials forced Vargas to resign from office.

General Eurico Gaspar Dutra was elected president in 1945. A new constitution was put in place that gave less control to the president. People wanted to prevent the possibility of another overpowering president like Vargas.

But in 1951, Vargas won a new election and became president again. Under the new constitution, Vargas could not lead as strongly as he had before World War II. Many of Vargas's supporters began to criticize him for weak leadership. In 1954, a group of military officers forced Vargas to resign from the presidency. Vargas then took his own life.

Period of Democracy

Under new president Juscelino Kubitschek, Brazil experienced a period of democracy. Kubitschek moved Brazil's capital from Rio de Janeiro to Brasília. Before this period, most Brazilians lived and worked in Rio de Janeiro and other areas within 200 miles (320 kilometers) of the coast. Kubitschek wanted to

▼ Brazil's capitol building is in Brasília. President Juscelino Kubitschek moved Brazil's capital from Rio de Janeiro to Brasília in 1960.

develop the country's resources farther inland. By moving the capital to Brasília, the president hoped to encourage settlement of the western region.

Under Kubitschek, Brasília grew quickly. Workers built roads and power plants. These actions brought industrial development to more areas of the country.

Despite the economic growth, many Brazilians still were poor. People moved from rural areas to

◄ President Fernando Henrique Cardoso is Brazil's current president.

coastal cities looking for jobs. Unable to find employment, these people moved to shantytowns outside Brazil's cities.

Beginning in 1960, Brazil underwent a period of political difficulty. Janio da Silva Quadros won the presidential election, while a supporter of Vargas, João Goulart, won the vice-presidential election. In 1964, the military again took control of Brazil's government until 1985. Citizens then elected José Samey as president and he declared Brazil a democracy.

Today, Brazil's government is stable. The current government under President Fernando Henrique Cardoso is trying to make Brazil a better place to live. The government's main goal is to provide strong and fair leadership that can serve all Brazilians peacefully.

Brazil's Modern Government

Today, Brazil is divided into 26 states and one federal district. Elections for state and federal offices are held every four years. Citizens ages 18 to 70 who can read are required by law to vote.

The government includes the executive, legislative, and judicial branches. The head of the executive branch is the president. The legislative branch consists of the Federal Senate and the Chamber of Deputies. The Federal Senate is made up of three elected members from each state and three from the federal district. Each state has three or more deputies in the Chamber of Deputies, depending on the state's population. There is a total of 513 deputies. The judicial branch is called the Supreme Federal Tribunal. The president appoints the judicial branch's 11 judges with the approval of the Senate.

Fast Facts about Brazil's Economy

System of weights and measures: metric system

Major types of industry: agriculture, forestry, manufacturing

Major natural resources/minerals: bauxite, gold, iron ore

Major agricultural products: coffee, soybeans, wheat, rice

Major types of manufactured products: automobiles, ships, synthetic fabrics and textiles, chemicals

Chief exports: manufactured goods, iron ore, soybeans, coffee

Chief imports: machinery and equipment, chemical products, oil, electricity

Chapter 4

Brazil's Economy

Brazil is one of today's leading industrial nations. The country produces many agricultural products and is rich in natural resources. The nation's farms, forests, and mines produce a wide variety of valuable exports. Brazil's factories and service industries greatly contribute to the country's economy, producing more goods and services each year than any other country in South America. The total value of all goods and services produced within Brazil each year is one of the highest in the world.

Manufacturing and Service Industries

Metal product manufacturing is Brazil's main industrial activity. South America's largest steel plant is located in Brazil. The nation also is one of the world's leading automobile manufacturers.

◄ This plant provides steel for Brazil's automobile factories.

Brazil's Industries and Natural Resources

KEY

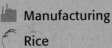

Coffee

G Gold

I Iron ore

M Manganese

Manufacturing

Rice

Soybeans

About 42 percent of Brazil's workers are employed in service jobs. Some of these people are teachers, health care workers, or government employees. Some hold jobs in banks, insurance agencies, and real estate agencies. Others work in transportation as pilots, flight attendants, and bus and taxi drivers.

Energy and Transportation

Brazil is able to meet most of its own energy needs. Hydroelectric power stations produce nearly all of Brazil's electricity. These large power plants operate by using flowing river water to make electricity.

Brazil produces about half of the oil it needs each year. Wells along the coast generate petroleum and natural gas. The rest of the oil is imported. The high cost of imported oil led Brazil to develop fuel made of alcohol. Brazilian farmers raise sugarcane, which can be made into alcohol. Many new automobiles in Brazil run entirely on alcohol. Brazil also uses coal and charcoal to meet its energy needs.

Mining and Forestry

Brazil has rich mineral deposits, including the largest iron ore deposits in the world. Most of these deposits are located in southeastern Brazil. The country has enough iron ore to meet Earth's iron needs for the next 500 years. Workers also mine Brazil's huge deposits of manganese, bauxite, nickel, and uranium. Brazil produces 90 percent of the world's gems, including amethyst, topaz, emerald, and aquamarine. Brazil is Earth's only source of high-quality quartz crystals. Rare black diamonds also have been found in Brazil.

Brazil is one of the world's leading producers of forest products. Loggers in southern Brazil cut down Paraná pine trees for timber, the country's main forest product. Workers make some of this timber into charcoal, an important fuel for many homes and industries. Brazil's forests are a source of other valuable products such as medicines, nuts, oils, rubber, and gum.

Agriculture and Fishing

Brazil is a world leader in agricultural production, with 31 percent of its population working in this industry. Approximately one-fourth of the world's coffee crop is grown in Brazil, mainly in the states of São Paulo and Minas Gerais. The country produces a variety of other crops, including oranges, papayas, bananas, lemons, sugarcane, and the world's largest crop of cassava. Brazil also is one of the world's top producers of cacao beans, cashews, corn, cotton, pineapples, rice, soybeans, and tobacco.

▼ This man dries coffee beans, one of Brazil's most important crops.

Brazilian farmers raise large supplies of livestock, including cattle, chickens, hogs, horses, and sheep. Brazilians consume most of the country's livestock. A small portion is exported.

Brazil's fishing industry is a major source of income. More than one-fourth of Brazil's freshwater fish come from the Amazon River. Lobster and shrimp make up most of the saltwater catch in Brazil.

Employment and Standard of Living

Brazil has a growing economy with a workforce of about 74 million people. The unemployment rate is only about 8.5 percent, but many workers labor long hours for low wages.

Brazil's wealth is distributed unevenly among its people. The wealthiest 10 percent earn half of the country's entire income. These wealthy Brazilians include some landowners, company leaders, and government officials. Business managers, government workers, and teachers also have a higher standard of living than most other Brazilians do.

Most Brazilians are very poor. Two-thirds of the country's workforce earn less than double the minimum wage. Brazil's challenge for today and the future is to reduce the number of people living in poverty.

The Brazilian unit of currency is the real. One real equals 100 centavos.

Currency exchange rates change every day. In the early 2000s, about 1.74 Brazilian reals equaled 1 U.S. dollar, and about 1.18 Brazilian reals equaled 1 Canadian dollar.

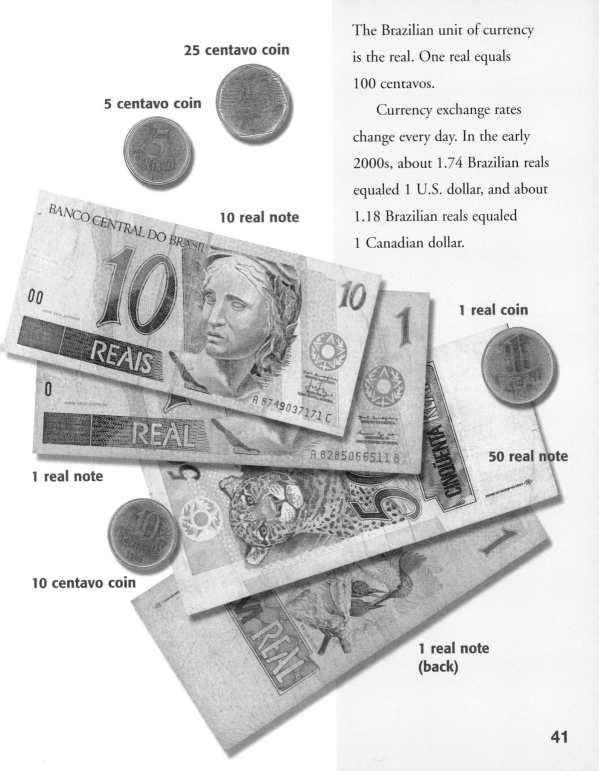

25 centavo coin

5 centavo coin

10 real note

1 real coin

1 real note

50 real note

10 centavo coin

1 real note (back)

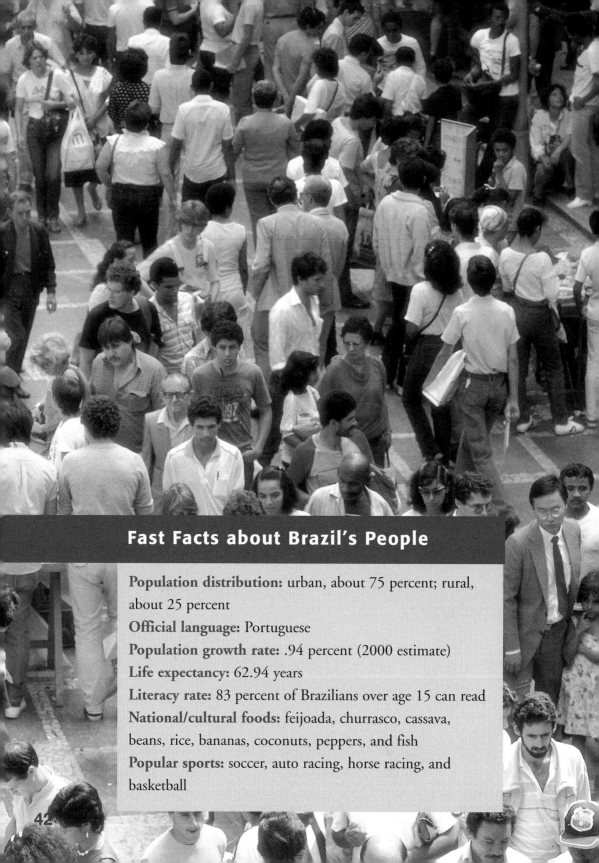

Fast Facts about Brazil's People

Population distribution: urban, about 75 percent; rural, about 25 percent

Official language: Portuguese

Population growth rate: .94 percent (2000 estimate)

Life expectancy: 62.94 years

Literacy rate: 83 percent of Brazilians over age 15 can read

National/cultural foods: feijoada, churrasco, cassava, beans, rice, bananas, coconuts, peppers, and fish

Popular sports: soccer, auto racing, horse racing, and basketball

Chapter 5

People, Culture, and Daily Life

Brazil is known as a country of acceptance. Brazilians of different ethnic backgrounds usually treat one another fairly. But ethnic background often decides a person's standard of living. Brazilians with European backgrounds usually are better educated and hold higher-level jobs in government and industry. Brazilians of native or African backgrounds often are very poor.

Ethnic Backgrounds and Language

Brazil has three major ethnic groups. People who have European ancestors make up about 55 percent of the nation's population. About 6 percent of the population is of African descent. People of mixed European and African backgrounds make up about 38 percent of the population.

◀ People of all backgrounds walk the busy streets of São Paulo.

Brazil's native population ranged between 2 million and 5 million at the time of the first European exploration. Today, fewer than 200,000 native peoples live in Brazil. Most of the native population lives in the Amazon region on government reserves. The largest reserve is the Yanomami Indigenous Park, which includes 37,066 square miles (96,000 square kilometers) of land. A small number of Brazilians, called caboclos, have mixed European and native backgrounds.

Portuguese is the official language of Brazil. Almost 100 percent of the population speaks the language. Native ethnic groups speak more than 90 traditional languages that are passed from generation to generation.

Religion

Ninety percent of Brazilians are Roman Catholic. The early Portuguese brought the Roman Catholic religion to Brazil. Today, Brazil has the largest number of Catholics in the world.

There are other religious groups in Brazil. About 5 percent of Brazil's people practice macumba and candomblé. These religions combine African spiritual beliefs and the Catholic faith. Protestants make up about 5 percent of Brazil's population. Lutherans form

▼ This statue, Christ the Redeemer, overlooks Rio de Janeiro. Ninety percent of Brazilians are Roman Catholic. Like other Christians, Roman Catholics believe Christ is the son of God.

▼ Many poor Brazilians live in slums called favelas, which are made up of cardboard, metal, or wood shacks.

the largest Protestant group. Brazil also has about 400,000 Buddhists and 150,000 Jews.

Living Conditions

The lifestyle in Brazil's cities is very different than it is in rural areas. About three-fourths of Brazil's population lives in cities. Wealthy city-dwellers enjoy modern conveniences and a fair standard of living. Their education allows them to find professional positions or good jobs in government. Other workers find jobs in banks, factories, offices, and stores.

Many poor Brazilians live in crowded city slums called favelas. Shacks made of cardboard, metal, or wood make up these neighborhoods. Residents do not have sewers or running water. Many people who live in favelas are unskilled workers who are unemployed or work for low wages. Many of these people suffer from disease and hunger.

About one-fourth of Brazil's population lives in rural areas. Many rural families live in small homes with few furnishings and often no modern conveniences. Only about 61 percent of the rural population has an adequate water supply. Sewers are available to only about 32 percent. Hunger and poverty are so common that most rural Brazilians can barely feed their families.

Learn to Speak Portuguese

Brazil is the only country in South America in which Portuguese is the official language.

good-bye—adeus (ah-day-OOS)

good day—bom dia (BOME GEE-uh)

hello—olá (oh-LA)

sorry—desculpe (DAY-skul-pay)

please—por favor (POR fuh-VOR)

no—não (NOU)

yes—sim (THIM)

Do you speak English?—
Fala inglês? (FAH-lah in-GLES)

thank you—obrigado
(oh-bree-GAWD-oh)

▲ Brazilian students learn to read and write Portuguese, the country's official language.

Women in Brazil

Brazilian women generally hold a lower status in society than men do. Women earn about 75 percent less than men who work at the same jobs. Many women lack a good education. Few women hold positions of power such as high-level government jobs. The poorest Brazilians are members of families headed by women.

But the status of Brazilian women is improving. Today, an equal number of boys and girls attend Brazilian schools, and more women are continuing their education. More women also are finding jobs in law, medicine, and engineering fields. Men usually dominate these fields.

Education

Children ages 7 through 14 are required by law to attend primary school. Brazil has both private schools and free public schools. Many upper-class and middle-class families pay to send their children to private schools. Many poor children drop out of the free public schools after primary school to help their families earn a living. Four more grades of middle school also are free to Brazilian children, but only about 10 percent of all students continue to this level of education. Most middle schools are located in the cities of the southeast. Many children do not have access to these schools.

About 83 percent of Brazil's adults are literate. They are able to read and write. But up to 60 percent of Brazilian adults have poor reading skills. They cannot read newspapers or write letters. The literacy rate is lowest in rural areas that have fewer schools and teachers. The government broadcasts school lessons over the radio in some regions. Students from universities sometimes volunteer to teach young students in rural areas.

Universities and colleges are free in Brazil. Many students want to attend college, but most students cannot. Students often cannot afford living expenses at faraway schools. Those who attend universities and colleges are mainly wealthy or upper middle-class.

Food and Clothing

Brazilians eat a variety of foods. Brazil's national dish, feijoada, is a combination of black beans, dried beef, and pork. Some Brazilian foods have a strong African influence. Many of these dishes contain bananas, coconuts, fish, and hot peppers. Charcoal-broiled meats called churrasco are popular in southern Brazil. Brazil's most important meat is beef. People also eat veal, pork, and chicken. Coffee is Brazil's main drink.

Make Negrinho

Brazilian children often make Negrinho to share with their friends at parties. Ask an adult to help you make this dessert.

What You Need

1 14-ounce (420-gram) can
   sweetened condensed milk
1 egg yolk
1 tablespoon (15 mL) butter
   or margarine
4 tablespoons (60 mL) sweetened cocoa
½ cup (125 mL) chocolate
   sprinkles, ground nuts, or shredded
   coconut for decoration
saucepan

wooden spoon
plate
measuring spoons
measuring cups

What You Do

1. In a saucepan over low heat, combine 1 14-ounce (420-gram) can of sweetened condensed milk and 1 egg yolk.
2. Stir mixture with a wooden spoon continually, until the mixture thickens and coats the spoon.
3. Stir in 1 tablespoon (15 mL) butter or margarine and 4 tablespoons (60 mL) sweetened cocoa.
4. Remove from heat and let the mixture cool.
5. With wet hands, form the mixture into small balls and roll them in chocolate sprinkles, ground nuts, or shredded coconut.
6. Serve on a plate and store leftovers in the refrigerator.

Makes 3 dozen cookies.

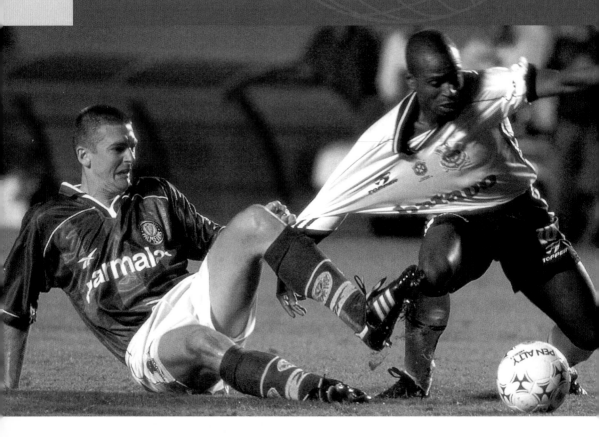

Brazilian clothing is a blend of Portuguese, African, and native peoples' influences. Some women of African background wear bright blouses and long, colorful skirts. Bracelets and necklaces accent this traditional clothing. The gauchos, or cowboys, of the south wear ponchos and baggy trousers called bombachas. Gauchos also wear wide-brimmed felt hats for protection from the sun. Other Brazilians wear clothing similar to clothing worn in the United States and Canada.

Sports and Pastimes

Brazil has 6,019 miles (9,686 kilometers) of coastline. The country's white, sandy beaches attract thousands of Brazilians and tourists every weekend. Many people enjoy fishing, skin diving, swimming, and boating along the Atlantic coast.

On land, other popular sports in Brazil include automobile racing, basketball, and horse racing. But soccer is Brazil's favorite sport. Brazilians call the game "futebol." Maracana Stadium in Rio de Janeiro is the world's largest stadium. Some soccer games there attract as many as 200,000 fans, and Brazilian soccer stars are treated as national heroes.

Brazil's Edson Arantes do Nascimento, known as Pelé, is the world's most famous soccer player. Pelé led the Brazilian soccer team to three World Cup victories and scored more than 1,000 goals before retiring in 1977.

Arts, Holidays, and Festivals

Many famous writers and artists were born in Brazil. Jorge Amado's humorous stories take place on plantations in the eastern state of Bahia. Gilberto

▲ People dress in elaborate costumes to celebrate Carnival, which is a blend of Brazilian and African traditions. This festival lasts four days.

Freyre wrote about life under slavery in Brazil. Brazilian artists such as Belmiro de Almeida Jr. and Cândido Portinari are well known for their portrayals of Brazilian native peoples and landscapes.

Brazilian dance music blends melodies from the past with music from the present day. This combination of European, African, and native sounds is popular throughout the country. Samba and bossa nova are two well-known types of Brazilian dance music that come from African music. In colonial times, slaves danced to the beat of African drums. Today, this heavy beat still is heard in Brazilian music.

Festivals are popular in Brazil. The best-known festival is Carnival, which is celebrated for four days before Lent each year. People in dazzling costumes ride on beautiful floats in parades. Dancers move to samba music on the streets. Dancing and celebrating continue all night long.

Brazilians observe other holidays. St. John's Night is celebrated in June with bonfires, fireworks, and paper hot-air balloons. Brazilians also observe Easter, Christmas, and New Year's Day. On September 7, Brazilians celebrate Independence Day and recognize the accomplishments of their country.

▲ Brazil has thousands of species of birds, including the toucan.

Brazil's National Symbols

◀ Flag

Brazil's flag was modified in 1992. The flag is green with a large yellow diamond in the center. Inside the diamond is a blue globe with 27 white stars, one star for each state and one for the federal district of Brasília. The stars are arranged in the same pattern as the night sky over Brazil. There is a white band across the globe with the words "Ordem E Progresso." These words mean "order and progress."

◀ Coat of Arms

Brazil's Coat of Arms was adopted in 1889. The large star represents unity and independence. The stars in the center of the coat of arms stand for the galaxy of the Southern Cross. The stars in the surrounding ring represent the states of Brazil. The garland is coffee leaves and tobacco leaves, two of Brazil's most important crops.

Other National Symbols

National Anthem: "Ouviram do Ipiranga as Margens Placidas" ("Heard from the Quiet Banks of the Ipiranga River")

National bird: golden parakeet

National dish: feijoada

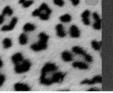

Timeline

A.D. 1494
Spain and Portugal sign the Treaty of Tordesillas.

1789
Brazilians lead a failed revolt against Portuguese rule.

1889
Brazil proclaims itself a republic.

1937
Getúlio Vargas becomes dictator.

| B.C. | A.D. | 1600 | 1800 | 1900 |

About 10,000 B.C.
The first people migrate to South America from Asia.

1500
Portuguese explorer Pedro Álvares Cabral lands in Brazil and claims it for his country.

1822
Brazil declares its independence from Portugal.

1930
The government is overthrown by military officials and Getúlio Vargas.

1942
Brazil declares war on the Axis powers during World War II (1939–1945).

1960
Brazil moves its capital from Rio de Janeiro to Brasília.

1995
Fernando Henrique Cardoso is elected president.

1950   **1980**   **2000**

1945
Vargas is removed from power.

1964
Military leaders take control of the government.

1985
Brazil's government is returned to civilian rule.

1946
A new constitution restores individual rights.

Words to Know

adobe (uh-DOH-bee)—a brick made of clay mixed with straw and dried in the sun

deforestation (dee-for-uh-STAY-shuhn)—the cutting down of forests

drought (DROUT)—a long period of time of very dry weather

favelas (fah-VAY-lahs)—slums where the houses are often made of cardboard or metal

pampas (PAM-puhz)—large, treeless plains in South America

plantation (plan-TAY-shuhn)—a large farm where crops such as coffee, tea, tobacco, and cotton are grown

poverty (POV-ur-tee)—the state of being poor

rain forest (RAYN FOR-ist)—a thick forest of tall trees and plants located in a warm, rainy climate

republic (ri-PUHB-lik)—a form of government in which the people have the power to elect representatives who manage the government; republics often have presidents.

samba (SAHM-bah)—Brazilian music with a heavy beat

savanna (suh-VAN-uh)—a flat, grassy plain with few or no trees; savannas are found in tropical areas.

To Learn More

Enderlein, Cheryl L. *Celebrating Birthdays in Brazil.* Birthdays around the World. Mankato, Minn.: Bridgestone Books, 1998.

Ferro, Jennifer. *Brazilian Foods and Culture.* Festive Foods and Celebrations. Vero Beach, Fla.: Rourke Press, 1999.

Heinrichs, Ann. *Brazil.* Enchantment of the World. New York: Children's Press, 1997.

Jermyn, Leslie. *Brazil.* Countries of the World. Milwaukee: Gareth Stevens Publishing, 1999.

Sirimarco, Elizabeth. *Yanomami.* Endangered Cultures. Mankato, Minn.: Smart Apple Media, 1999.

Useful Addresses

Consulate General of Brazil—Toronto, Canada

77 Bloor Street West

Suites 1109 & 1105

Toronto, ON M5S 1M2

Canada

Embassy of Brazil

3006 Massachusetts Avenue NW

Washington, DC 20008

Internet Sites

Altapedia Online—Brazil

http://www.atlapedia.com/online/countries/brazil.htm

A summary and maps of Brazil

Brazilian Embassy in Washington

http://www.brasilemb.org

Information on Brazil's economy, tourism, environment, and more

CIA—The World Factbook (Brazil)

http://www.odci.gov/cia/publications/factbook/geos/br.html

Statistics and basic information on Brazil

Oxfam Cool Planet's Brazil

http://www.oxfam.org.uk/coolplanet/kidsweb/world/Brazil/
       brazhome.htm

History, geography, people, and fast facts

▼ Brazilian families eat a variety of foods at meals. Many drink soda or coffee as a beverage.

65

Index